MW01277682

BEEKEEPING STARTER GUIDE

THE COMPLETE USER GUIDE TO KEEPING BEES, RAISE YOUR BEE COLONIES AND MAKE YOUR HIVE THRIVE IN YOUR BACKYARD OR GARDEN

OLIVIA COOPER

© 2020 Olivia Cooper

You are welcome to join the

Fan's Corner, here

Beekeeping Starter Guide

The Complete User Guide to Keeping Bees, Raise Your Bee Colonies and Make your Hive Thrive in your Backyard or Garden

Olivia Cooper

Disclaimer

The advice and strategies found within may not be suitable for every situation. This work is sold with the understanding that neither the author nor the publisher is held responsible for the results accrued from the advice in this book.

Table of Content

INTRODUCTION

Apiculture is an aspect of agriculture that is primarily concerned with the practice of managing, maintaining, and keeping bees, their colonies, and their hives. The entire bee colony ecosystem that consists of the royal jelly, raw honey, and beeswax is known as the Apiary. Apart from being sustainable, good for health, these products are also very much sought.

If you are just a beginner and have ever had thoughts of keeping your bees, then this beekeeping book is for you. In this book specifically written for adults who are interested in natural beekeeping and need a book that not only explains the basics of beekeeping for the beginner but also shows how to manage the business side of keeping bees to make it a profitable business churning out profit consistently.

So, if all you wanted was to be a backyard beekeeper or a hobbyist or simply a small-time farmer hoping to use his homestead to start a business selling honey and other bee products, this guide which has pictures to illustrates the point has been designed to get you started in no time, and you know what, it's fairly easy to learn the process of managing how to keep bees.

As with many other aspects of life, many factors come into play before deciding to embark on a beekeeping adventure, so before you dive right in, you may want to first consider if keeping bees is suitable for you.

That means that the first step to the long journey of becoming a successful keeper of bees is to acquire as much knowledge as possible about the bees to acquaint yourself with all the potential variables that have the capacity to affect the outcome of your honey bees.

This beginner's pack will show you how to select your hive for your first beehive, help you prepare for possible challenges you may face in the future. Each day you go out to see your bees can become a new experience in itself as you get to see something different every time you get into your hive, this book was written to make each beekeeping experience an interesting one for you.

To be able to make appropriate management decisions, especially when preparing to start commercial beekeeping, it is important to know the importance of being flexible in your approach and to develop an uncanny ability to figure out your bees act the way they do at one time and then turn around to behave in a totally different way at other times. The ability to differentiate each of these supposedly simple actions and how those actions can impact their wellbeing is what usually differentiates a successful beekeeper from a failed beekeeping practice.

So, ride along with us as we expose and simplify the aspects of beekeeping for you in a language that is simple to understand.

CHAPTER 1

ABOUT BEES

Bees are insects that fly and are similar to ants and wasps. Bees come from the monophyletic origin within the Apoidea family. There are more than 20,000 recognized species of bees that are recognized in seven families. Some of the bee species live in colonies socially e.g.

bumblebees, honey bees, and stingless bees while other species like carpenter bees, leafcutter bees, mason bees, and sweat bees prefer to live separately.

Bees exist in every environment that is surrounded by insect-pollinated flowering plants in all the continents except Antarctica. Bees vary in sizes as some species are tiny and stingless with workers that are less than 2 millimeters (0.08 in) long, and some like the largest specie (Megachile pluto) of leafcutter bee, have females that can be as long as 39 millimeters. Nectar and pollen are what bees feed on. The nectar serves as a source of energy to the bees and pollen gives protein and other nutrients. The bee larvae also feed on pollen.

Bee has both insect predators like dragonflies and bird predators like bee-eaters.

TYPES OF BEE SPECIES

There are approximately 25,000 species of bees globally. Furthermore, the 25,000 species are further categorized into more than 4000 types of bees (genera) which relate within 9 superfamilies (Apoidea). Additionally, there are approximately 4000 species in the US, and there are above 250 species in Britain and likely more species to be known. Here are the types of bees classified by family:

Apidae: Examples of bees in this family are stingless bees, honeybees, and bumblebees.

Megachilidae: These are usually solitary bees like the mason bees and the Leafcutter bee.

Andrenidae: This family is a wide bee specie family with the andrena genera and 1300 other bee species. They are mining bees

Colletidae: They include approximately 2000 species including the yellow-faced bees and plasterers.

Halictidae: They are smallish bees usually referred to as sweat bees. They are usually dark-colored with some yellow, red, or green stripes.

Mellittidae: They are a small family of Africa bees with about 60 species in 4 genera.

Meganomiidae: They are a small bee family in Africa with about 10 species in 4 genera.

Dasypodaidae: They comprise over 100 species in 8 genera.

Stenotritidae: This is a small bee family found in Australia with about 21 species in 2 genera. They were initially a part of the colletidae family.

The most common types of bees are honey bees, bumblebees, killer bees, mason bees leafcutter, and carpenter bees.

HONEY BEES (APIDAE)

Honey bees are categorized as 'social bees' because they can live in colonies that have about 50,000 – 60,000 workers. There are 10 varieties of honey bee globally, and one hybrid bee known as the Africanized bee. The European honey bee is generally reared and harvested by beekeepers in the West. Honey bees are also broadly used by other bees in pollinating crops.

Honeybees can be seen anywhere in the world and they have large families. The honeybee is the sole social insect whose colony can exist for a long time. And this happens because they gather, and nestle together, and eat honey to stay alive during the winter season. Honeybees pollinate over 100 food crops in the U.S. Their wings flutter about 11,000 times each minute, that's why they sound like they are "buzzing". Honeybees usually also sting, but they do that only once. This is because their stingers are barbed and tear off whenever they leave. The sting can be very painful if the stinger is not instantly extracted from the person which can sometimes result in a terrible reaction to persons allergic to insect stings.

Honey bees have a golden yellow color with brown bands. Honeybees use the pollen and nectar of plants to make honey. They reserve the honey in honeycombs in their hives, and they feed the honey to their young ones during the winter. Honeybee nests differ in size. They generally construct their nests in the crevices of trees, and sometimes they build it in attics or chimneys.

BUMBLEBEES (APIDAE)

Bumblebees are seen as beneficial insects because they are great pollinators of numerous types of plants and food crops. Their excellence as pollinators is partly related to the furry shape of their body and also their capacity to 'buzz pollinate'. They are extremely social bees that exist in large "families". The bumblebee is different from the honeybee because they have smooth stingers that don't stick to the skin when the move away so they can sting severally. The bumblebee sting is very painful and can cause swelling and irritation which can linger for days.

Bumblebees are black in color with yellow stripes. Bumblebees collect nectar and pollen, then use it to feed their larvae and other bees in the colony. Most of the bumblebee colonies are relatively small, with about 50 to 400 workers, but you can expect them to be typically around 120 to 200. Bumblebees usually build their nest on the floor, but sometimes they set up their nests above the ground around decks or balcony areas. Sometimes they also set up their nests in attics or under the beam of roofs. When they are agitated, they normally buzz loudly, and they aggressively and boldly protect and guard their nests. As part of the hostile protection of their nests, bumblebees will pursue nest invaders for a long period of time and long distances.

KILLER BEES

Africanized killer bees are similar to the normal honeybees physically, but they have varied wing measurements. Africanized bees stay in South America and the Western and Southern United States. They are recognized for chasing people over a quarter of a mile when they are angry. Though they are usually referred to as "killer" bees, their venom is not more toxic than the normal honeybees. Yet, these bees usually attack in groups, which makes them more dangerous to humans, particularly to allergic people. Africanized "killer" bees can only sting once because their stingers are not smooth and tear off when they try to fly away. They have a golden yellow color with darker bands of brown. Killer bees collect nectar and pollen, then to serve as food to the colony and their larvae. Africanized bees usually own little colonies, which means they can set up their nests in unusual places like boxes, crates, empty cars, tires, etc. It is advisable to move in a zigzag style if attacked by Africanized bees and seeks refuge in a building or a vehicle. Also, be careful when dealing with stuff that could surround an Africanized bee nest.

CARPENTER BEES AND DIGGER BEES (Apidae)

Carpenter bees are solitary bees. They set up nests and feed only themselves and their young ones. They possess the ability to bore through wood and that's how they got their name. They have smooth stingers so they can sting several times. They are blue-black in color. These bees collect nectar and pollen to give to their young ones as food. Carpenter bees drill through delicate woods to lay their eggs and safeguard their larvae as they evolve. Female bees can chew a tunnel into bits of wood to set up a nested path. The pieces of wood she chews and keep outside the nest are called "frass". The opening of the passage is normally around one or two inches deep, and they have a length of up to 10 feet long. These tunnels normally have various rooms where the bees keep their eggs and store their food.

Carpenter bees are not life-threatening, but they can destroy the wood where they set up their nests. Carpenter bees are useful because they pollinate plants that are ignored by honeybees.

DIGGER BEES

Digger bees are solitary bees and great pollinators as well. Digger bees normally set up their nests in the soil. They possess hairy bodies and can be as long as 3cm. Some species in the US, for instance, can possess a brown ginger-like, body with hairs, or possess black glossy trunks.

LEAF CUTTER BEES AND MASON BEES

These bees are also solitary. Normally with solitary bees, a solitary female mate, then builds a nest independently, and takes care of the larvae. Nevertheless, some solitary bees, do exist in a simple societal structure or social group where a few solitary bees may build their nests near one another, and in some instances, they even ration guarding of the nests and scouring for food duties.

Mason bees like to set up their nests in crevices, and Leafcutter bees prefer hollow stems and holes in wood. Leafcutter bees cut away portions of leaves for building their egg cells. Leafcutter bees do not damage the plant from which it takes the part from the leaf. Solitary bees rearing for commercial bee pollination are rising.

MINING BEES (ANDRENIDAE)

Mining bees are related to a big family of bees made entirely of numerous kinds of bees around the world. Mining bees are also solitary, the females make nests closely with each other. Mining bees dig tunnels and cells under the soil. They are visible in yards, gardens, small ridges and heaps of earth in fields, or even in borders. Generally, they appear to like sandy soil. They don't cause a lot of damage and can be accepted in the garden. They are also an important source of pollinators of plants and flowers.

PLASTERER BEES

Plasterer bees can also be called cellophane bees, and sometimes even polyester bees. These bees make amazing glues.

WOOL CARDER BEES

This lovely wool carder bee collects plant hairs, wraps them into small balls, and utilizes them to make its nest.

FLOWER BEES

Flower bees are great to plant pollinators.

NOMAD BEES

The Nomad bees can easily be misinterpreted as tiny wasps. Nomad bees are cleptoparasites.

STINGLESS BEES

The Stingless bees are wonderful bees that pollinate flowers. Surprisingly, some stingless bee species feed on dead meat!

LONG-HORNED BEES

These are bees with long antennae visibly obvious in the male bees.

FURROW BEES

Furrow bees scour for food on wildflowers such as knapweeds and thistles.

TYPES OF BEES IN A HIVE

There are several types of bees in a beehive: Queen, Worker, and Drone. Each of these kinds of bees has its vital functions and does certain duties in a colony.

THE QUEEN

Queen bees are differentiated from the other bees in the hive by their long abdomens and small wings. The queen's abdomen is normally sleek-smooth and long, extending beyond her folded wings. Sometime after their birth, they go out to mate with 15 or more drones over a

21

three-day term before they retreat to the colony to lay eggs.

The queen will remain in the hive and not leave again unless the colony requires a new home. The queen's duty in the hive is to reproduce. She is usually the only reproductive female in the colony as there is one queen bee per hive. She lays eggs in the early spring when the first new pollen is brought by the workers to the colony. She continues to produce eggs as long as the pollen is available.

The Queen can lay as much as 2000 eggs each day. A queen bee's life span barely exceeds 2-3 years, but she can survive for up to 7 years. Younger queens generate multiple eggs, and older ones may produce many drones. Most beekeepers replace their queens every year or two. Aging and older queens are continuously replaced by the workers without any assistance.

When the colony wants another queen bee, they just select a healthy larva that has already been hatched from an egg of the existing queen and give it royal jelly (a special and super nutritious food) to feed on. The royal jelly enables the larva to grow into a Queen. A professional beekeeper can rear good queens, but a beginner will just buy good queens from a reliable producer. Queen bees also produce a pheromone referred to as queen substance.

This chemical combination is individually transferred from one bee to another bee throughout the full hive as they share food. If a queen bee leaves a colony, the worker bees usually discover her absence within some hours because the pheromone level will drop. This state of having no Queen will promptly activate the desire to get a new "emergency" queen from the youngest usable larvae (1-3 days old). This emergency situation can also limit the development of the ovaries of the workers. After a period of having no queen, some of the workers may become laying workers. Workers also assess their queen based on the amount of the pheromones she produces. If workers start getting limited or inadequate doses each day, they may see her as a low-quality queen, and begin to prepare to replace her. Beekeepers usually mark the queen's thorax with color to be able to locate her easily and to know if she has been replaced.

WORKER BEES

Workers are the smallest bees in the bee colony, and they are the most numerous. The workers are female, and typically unable to reproduce. They are not able to mate, but in a circumstance where there is no queen in the colony, workers may start laying unfertilized eggs, which later become drones. Worker bees comprise about 99% of the entire bee population of each colony and they are the most familiar members.

The worker bee's stinger is barbed, so when she is compelled to protect herself or the hive, her stinger tears off if she flies away because her stinger will be stuck on the sufferer's skin. She dies when she inevitably rips herself away from the stuck stinger. The stinger left behind will continue to put venom from the venom sack into her victim.

Workers have 3 simple eyes that consist of the vertex and fully developed compound eyes on each side of their heads. Their tongue is nicely developed and extended for taking nectar from flowers. Worker bees do nearly everything for the hive. From the birth of the worker bee to her death, which is roughly 45 days later, the worker is assigned several duties to perform during the various phases of her life. Worker bees perform the function of:

- Cleaning the hive

- Producing the royal jelly used to feed their queen and their larva

- Building honeycombs by secreting the wax used in the hive and molding it into honeycombs.

- Collecting the food by foraging for nectar and pollen, bringing it to the hive, and converting the nectar to honey.

- Tending to the demands of the larvae and queens.

- Capping the cells of mature larvae for pupation and removing debris and lifeless bees from the hive.

- Guarding and defending the hive against enemies and conserve optimal conditions If the hive by warming, cooling, and airing the hive.

Workers raised during spring and early summer season live for about five to six weeks. In the first two weeks of their lives, they spend it as house bees performing tasks in the hive. For the remaining part of their life span, they spend it as field bees, foraging for food outside the hive.

DRONES

Drones are the male honey bees whose purpose is in mating with and fertilizing a young queen bee. If they get the chance to mate, they die shortly afterward. If they don't mate, they can survive for up to 90 days. Drones are easily recognized in the hive by their big round bodies and large eyes. They are bigger in size and stouter than workers. They have big distinct eyes that unite at the top of their heads and possess antennae a little bit longer than that of the queen or workers. They have a reduced mouth part. Drones come from unfertilized eggs, and the cells of drones are larger than that of workers.

Drones feed themselves directly from honey in the hive or get food from worker bees. They are reared mainly in the spring and summer, starting about four weeks before new queens are generated, therefore making sure that sufficient drones will be prepared to mate with new queens. Their day is normally split between eating times and resting times, and guarding mating sites called drone congregation areas. As the number of accessible food decreases, drone production will stop in the late summer. Before winter, the drones are normally sent out of the hive by workers, who guard the hives, so they won't come back. A colony without a queen may create laying workers, who can bring forth just drones. When this happens, the colony will be in bad condition. The production of many drones, hence, will be their last step to pass on the genetic line of the colony by mating with a virgin queen from another colony.

THE HIVE

Honeybees do not create an exterior layout that surrounds their hive. They love staying in hollow areas like a hollow tree, a deserted fallen wood, or in a regular man-made beehive.

Nevertheless, they construct the interior part of their hive. Honeybees produce beeswax, which the bees utilize to construct excellent small hexagons inside their hive. Smaller openings are called cells, then the bees keep everything, including eggs, pollen, and honey in them. They make a substance referred to as propolis to close and cover their hive and also, to defend them against diseases. Propolis includes a mixture of beeswax, plant resins, and honey. It is also anti-fungal, anti-bacterial, and anti-viral.

Beeswax is sticky and the bees use it to cover gaps or openings they may experience during housekeeping, it further sterilizes and safeguards their home. Due to the large population in the colony, they require a form of communication to understand each other. Bees communicate in two ways: by scent and by dancing. Whenever a bee is warning the other bees about an enemy, when the bees inside the hive are especially delighted, honeybees can expel a particular hormonal aroma known as the pheromones. The honeybees normally recognize these scents and understand their message. A happy bee pheromone has a lemon fragrance, and a warning smell has the scent of a banana. A bee that is foraging wants to give notice to her sisters as to where to get nectar, then she dances. She performs unique turns and wiggles drawing a map to indicate where she got the food.

THE EGGS AND DEVELOPMENT STAGES OF A BEE

The development stages of bees begin with eggs. In the winter, a queen establishes a new colony by laying eggs in every cell inside the honeycomb. The fertilized eggs then hatch into female worker bees, while unfertilized eggs will evolve into drones or honey bee males. For a colony to stand, the queen must lay fertilized eggs that will become worker bees, which will get food and take care of the duties in the colony.

Every colony has only one queen, which mates early and gathers over 5 million sperm cells. A honey bee queen goes out to mate and keeps sufficient sperm during the mating flight that will enable her to lay eggs throughout her lifetime. When a queen can't lay eggs anymore, a new queen mate and start laying the eggs. The approximate magnitude of the egg of a honey bee ranges from 1-1.5 millimeters in height, which is half of the size of one grain of rice. The egg is usually oblong in shape, a little bit curved and tapering at the end of one side. Before eggs are laid by the queen bee, the queen goes through the honeycomb, and assess each cell before she lays her eggs. The time used in laying a single egg is just some seconds, and the queen bee can lay about two thousand eggs in a day.

A young queen bee places the eggs using a systematic pattern, positioning each egg close to the others within a cell. Queens start laying their eggs in the middle of the cell structure so that workers can position honey, royal jelly, and other foods for larvae on the edges. Nevertheless, the number of eggs a queen lays begins to reduce as she ages. Whenever an egg is laid by the queen, a mucous strand attaches it to the hive cell by a mucous thread.

In the first development phase, the digestive, and nervous system, and outer covering forms. Three days later, the eggs develop into larvae. The worker bees feed honey, royal jelly, and other plant liquids to the larvae. These honey bee larvae possess no legs, eyes, antennae, or wings; they possess a small mouth and are similar to a single rice grain. Then, they feed and develop into adult workers, queens, or drones.

LIFE CYCLE OF A BEE

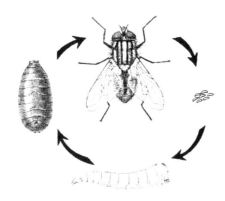

The stages of the life of a solitary or social bee entail the complete development of a bee from the laying of an egg, to the development of a legless larva, to the pupation stage where the insect completely undergoes metamorphosis and the emerging of an adult bee.

Most solitary bees and bumblebees develop in spring when many flowering plants come into bloom. The males are usually the first to emerge and then they look for females to mate with. The bee's sex depends on the fertilization. After the female bee is mated with, the female keeps the sperm and specifies the required sex at the time an egg is laid. The fertilized eggs produce female bees and the unfertilized eggs produce male bees. Bees in tropical regions typically generate several generations in a year.

The larvae of most bee species are white grubs, having a slightly oval shape, and bluntly-tapering at the ends of the egg. They possess fifteen segments. Also, they have spiracles for breathing in each of the segments. They don't have legs but move inside the cell on their sides.

They possess horns on their crown, an appendage on one part of their mouth with bristle jaws for eating. They have a gland under their mouth that emits a viscous liquid which hardens into the silk used in producing a cocoon. The pupa can be visibly observed through the cocoon as the cocoon is slightly transparent. After some days, the larva then develops into a winged adult. When the adult is prepared to come out, it divides its skin dorsally, goes out, and pulls away from the cell.

CHAPTER 2

WHY BEEKEEPING IS IMPORTANT

On a larger picture, a lot of people know the value of bees instinctively. Bees have an essential role to play in the natural environment and we know that if bees are no longer around, an ecological void in which other species can't take their place would be created. There are great reasons why beekeeping is so important:

1. Bees make honey

One of the purposes of beekeeping is to get honey. Bees make honey and beeswax. Honey is really useful to us. Honey is fantastic on toast, ice cream, and ham, fresh out of the oven. It can be useful in adding more flavor to your tea and coffee. Also, some people rear bees simply because they love honey, the same way people keep chickens because they love eggs.

2. Beekeeping is relatively cheap

Getting started with beekeeping is not so expensive. What you have to do is to either buy an established hive or bee kit and the materials to arrange your hives. Also, you would have to put in funds in a bee suit and get cleaning and harvesting tools. After you make that preparatory expense, you won't need to spend much to maintain the hive. Beekeeping is also pretty economical when compared to non-agrarian vocations.

For example, a hobby like golf has nonstop expenditures. Your early expenses may be minor if you don't spend much on clubs and balls, but every game you play you will spend a little bit more. You could have more expenses in one particular season than the expenses a new beekeeper would spend on building hives. In the next season, you will spend even more. Which adds up in the long run. Some hobbies are more expensive than beekeeping, so beekeeping is a reasonably impressive choice if you're thinking of an affordable hobby or vocation that you can do.

3. Beekeeping is interesting

People like to adopt hobbies they discover to be both delightful and relaxing. It is delightful to put on the bee suit and clean the hives. There is a unique feeling about managing hives early in the mornings or in the cool evenings. Also, keeping bees allows you a time of relaxation as you can tend to bees at least once a week.

4. Beekeeping is rewarding

Keeping bees is rewarding to beekeepers starting with the chance to support in reviving the falling population of bees as a result of CCD. Bee populations are gradually rising again as a result of the efforts beekeepers put in around the world and this is a reasonable reason to encourage beekeepers to keep rearing bees.

5. Beekeeping provides a relationship with nature

Industrialization and urbanization have developed different countries around the globe. Beekeeping relates to the beekeeper with the natural environment. Society needs to reconnect with nature if we want to save and maintain the earth. Beekeeping teaches people to enjoy nature and appreciate how to preserve it.

6. Bees are useful in your garden

Beekeeping is useful for trees and plants. Bees are pollinators. Keeping hives in your yard will be great for your plants.

7. Beekeeping is enlightening

Beekeeping is a highly enlightening vocation as well. The learning doesn't stop. Beekeeping learning starts with studying the differences between starter hives and bee kits. Then you continue to learn about queens, workers, and drones. Also, you learn the life cycle of a bee, and how the life cycle influences the health and productivity of a hive. In the following year, you will learn how diseases affect colonies, how to identify the symptoms of illnesses and diseases, and what to do when they come. So, in general, you basically have to know everything from the life of bees to how bees behave to prevent the colony from collapsing.

8. Bees are pollinators

Bees have a primary function that contributes to balance the ecosystem which is pollination. Bees carry pollen from one plant to the next. Pollinators are critical to the existence of plant life. Nature has formulated several means of performing pollination. But honeybees are by far the best pollinators. They go out into a garden in search of food then they take it to the hive. They fly from one flower plant to another flower, taking pollen and compressing it into compressed balls. Each time they settle on another flower, some of the balls they collected drops into the flower's reproductive canal. This is what makes flowers to sprout and grow. Studies have shown that honeybees account for over 30% of food crops in the world.

9. You can earn money from keeping bees

You can earn a little more money by keeping bees. Some of the extra money you get can come from agriculturists who wish to take your beehives every season. Planters and farmers need beehives for pollination, and they are ready to spend a decent amount of money to borrow beehives to help them enhance the productivity of their crops. Some professional beekeepers earn a decent living from just renting hives to agriculturists that need it.

10.   Agriculture relies on bees

Agricultural aspects including both crops and animal husbandry depend on bees. The valuable service bees add to the natural experiment, create a possibility for ranches, farms, and cattle rearing to prosper because, without bees, the farms would suffer. A lot of crops are reliant on pollination from bees. Also, bees pollinate clover and alfalfa which are used to graze cattle and different livestock. A scarcity in clover and alfalfa would make it hard to rear and sustain the animals. Apart from the commercial aspect of agriculture, bees further pollinate the plants, flowers, and trees that naturally exist.

11. To save the falling bee population

Most beekeepers take dignity and satisfaction in beekeeping realizing that they are helping to balance the decreasing bee populations. Sadly, several factors have combined over the previous twenty years to seriously reduce bee populations around the world. Beekeeping is great because it enhances the action to increase bee populations.

12. The knowledge of beekeeping is gradually fading away

One factor that contributes to the declining bee population is the fact that people no longer take beekeeping as a job. There is no difference between growing crops or raising cattle as beekeeping has been around for years. The issue with beekeeping is that it is not performed on an industrial basis. Beekeeping is particularly labor-intensive. And because bees are so subtle, it is extremely hard for beekeepers to pursue incredibly massive operations on an equivalent scale as an industrial farm. The truth is that professional and experienced beekeepers are leaving and passing away. The death of every beekeeper signifies the standard of beekeeping knowledge disappearing from global awareness. And without adequate new beekeepers coming in to carry on with beekeeping, there is nobody to get the knowledge from them. Beekeeping is a highly professional process that employs a balanced technique, understanding, and skill. It can't be easily industrialized. If we keep allowing the knowledge and experience of beekeeping to perish with those beekeepers who have it, we could get to the point where most people wouldn't know how to rear bees and it will be overwhelming if any severe occurrences of colony collapse disorder happen in such situation. It will be extremely challenging for us to raise the population of beehives both the bees that are being managed and the wild bees if we can't motivate inexperienced and young people to begin keeping bees.

13. Bees are part of the food distribution system

Beekeeping is also important to the universal food chain. There are two things to evaluate here, starting with the fact that honeybees have biological predators. Bees are prey to other species of animals like small birds, mammals, reptiles, and even other insects because of their small sizes. The falling population of bees is detrimental to these different predators because of the relative decrease in the supply of their food. If there isn't a decent number of bees to meet up with the need for food, those predators start looking for supplementary food. This affects the natural food chain. Another thing to note is that bees contribute to both human and animal food supplies. Bees pollinate plants and a collapse in bee populations will make it difficult for farmers to grow crops. Additionally, the grains we use in feeding farm animals are pollinated by bees. The reducing bee population also affects the food supply of herbivorous animals since plants rely on pollination to germinate.

14.   Bees are dependent on humans

Humans are the intelligent species that have the intelligence to relate science to the current situation. Humans are distinct in the sense we have knowledge that we can apply to situations. Humans possess the ability to discover strategies to enable the survival of other species. This ability is one of the various potentials that makes us so distinct from other creatures. Humans possess the capacity to preserve and increase the falling bee population.

SOCIO-ECONOMIC IMPORTANCE OF BEEKEEPING

It is generally believed that one-third of the food that we eat each day depends on pollination by bees especially. Several local and imported fruits and vegetables, flowers, and food crops need pollination. For example, apples, pears, field beans, runner and dwarf beans, strawberries, blueberries, raspberries, blackberries, and commercial crops rely entirely on bees. As a result of rising bee activity in the area which boosts the crop, the crop can gain indirectly from being in a habitat where bees exist even if the crop isn't directly pollinated by the bees. Honey bees can also pollinate clover and alfalfa, which are eaten by cattle, so bees are important to the meat and dairy industry also. It's essential to rear bees for honey production. Honeybees play an important part in pollinating other valuable crops like cotton and flax. Bees are also important for the generation of beeswax (which are used in beauty products and cleaning), propolis, pollen (bee bread), royal jelly, and bee venom (used for food, medicine, and income).

CHALLENGES OF BEEKEEPING

Beekeeping is a practice that comes with difficulties in running it. Common challenges in beekeeping include:

1. Not certain of where to get knowledge

Just like every vocation, beekeeping is a skill-based venture and requires some form of training to understand how to run it. Therefore, it is crucial to gain a certain level of understanding before starting. Prior knowledge and understanding save your time, capital, and more critically help your bees to be strong. Beekeeping is an ancient activity that has been passed on from one generation to generation. Presently, people are more confident because they have the privilege of reading and knowing everything we want to know or even acquire an online beekeeping course before starting the beekeeping practice. Beekeeping practice requires continuous learning because beekeeping usually has its difficulties, and regardless of the level of experience. Something to learn about like a nectar dearth, a disease, weather factor, or even market challenges is always there. To get knowledge on beekeeping, you can take a course on beekeeping or join a beekeeper's association and establish a network with experienced beekeepers.

2. Challenges encountered in your first bee colony

Getting bees for the first colony can be a challenge to beekeepers who are just starting. A few ways to get bees for a start are:

- Buying nuc locally

- Trapping wild swarms

- Buying already packaged bees

Trapping the swarms individually isn't a great option for beginners, except they have an experienced beekeeper to assist them because the experience can be quite frightening and discouraging for beginners. The easiest option for beginners to acquire bees is to buy a nuc locally from other beekeepers. In this case, the bees will not pass through the stress of being shipped and the beekeeper has a fellow beekeeper he can meet when he needs assistance.

3. Confused about where to place a beehive

Determining and choosing a location for the beehive is a common challenge a new beekeeper may have especially in recent times where there are climate changes, chemical substances, and the economy has a substantial influence on our activities. New beekeepers usually place the beehive in their yard.

This is only convenient if they live in the outskirts of the city, but if they reside within the city and are surrounded by neighbors, or close to an avenue, it may be challenging for them because beehives shouldn't be located where it can easily cause a likely threat and risk to other people, animals or bees themselves. A location with good floral is a good place for bees. Also, the location should be able to protect the bees from predators and destroyers, possess a close source of water with drainage and adequate sunlight.

4. Floral source needed for bees

There are approximately 20000 species of bees worldwide, and the honey bee is just one of the species. Several types of honey bees develop to pollinate the species of plants in their biological environment. For instance, in Italy, the bees are lured to citrus flowers. If there was no citrus flower in their habitat, the bee will avoid other flowers. The Africanized bees, for example, will not survive if they are taken to the south of Brazil to pollinate Eucalyptus because they usually pollinate the Amazonas. Understanding plant species and native species will be useful in beekeeping practice.

5. Handling queen bees

A beehive can't stay without its Queen. Usually, most beekeepers who are just starting can't tell when their colony has no queen. Usually, because they think that the behavior of the colony will normally change. So, when the colony has no queen, they won't realize it.

There are usually lots of honey and traffic at the opening of the beehive because the workers will devote all their time to forage for food since there are no larvae to take care of. By the time the beekeeper discovers that the bee population has decreased in numbers, and the colony has been without a queen for too long, it could be too late, and the colony dies.

A queen produces up to 2000 eggs in a single day.

A queenless colony is recognized when there is no new generation during the warm season. Another thing that can occur is that an old queen can be wavering, and not producing sufficient eggs as she did before, or the colony seems to be behaving differently, or, the colony is unproductive. These are indications and hints that the Queen needs to be replaced.

There are many means of replacing a queen. Just generally have a relatively elevated probability of approving a new queen. The bees themselves can even make it easier for you by deciding themselves and choosing a new queen for themselves. If you are initiating a new queen, make sure that the old queen is already dead or gone one day before initiating the new queen. If you waste time before introducing the new queen, the workers will begin to lay eggs that are not fertilized and will develop into drones later.

6. The health of your bee colony

Beekeeping is difficult sometimes, as it requires continuous learning. Some degrees of occasional deaths of colonies cannot be averted. But maintaining a healthy beehive is a significant factor in beekeeping. People have taken European honey bees around the world, and the bees have contacted strange diseases. And as beekeepers transferred their colonies through diverse location, infections and parasites circulate everywhere. The Varroa mite is a major problem of beekeepers and bees worldwide.

This parasite sticks to the bees and suck their blood and weaken the bees until they die. They spread too fast round the colonies and apiaries. They have a high ability to reproduce and this makes them dangerous and challenging for beekeepers. Some other parasites to the bees are small hive beetles, wax moths, the foulbrood, nosema, chalkbrood, the sacbrood virus, and some diseases like the deformed wing virus.

These parasites, infections, and diseases are a consistent problem for beekeepers, and it is certainly essential to know how to manage the health of the bees in a colony because it will determine their wellbeing.

Maintaining a bee colony has a natural health significance and every beekeeper has distinct ways of managing it. One thing to note is that low and poor management practices result in a low impact. A few good management tips are:

- Do not integrate a colony that is collapsing with a healthy colony.

- Do not use the same equipment used in a collapsing or sick colony in another colony without sterilizing the equipment.

- Decrease the degree of how exposed your colonies are to pesticides.

- Study and get information about the useful management practices that successful beekeepers use.

7. Honey prices and market demand

For beekeepers who keep bees for profit, the primary reason why most of them discontinue beekeeping is that the expenses and costs can become higher than the price of the product. Therefore, the main explanation of why a beekeeper stops beekeeping is because the market can sometimes displace them.

For instance, 30% of beekeepers who were one of the great local exporters of honey in Uruguay, discontinued the activity. Those who take beekeeping as a means of recreation may not have this problem. However, later on, they may generate more honey than they can eat or consume and might wish to trade some of the honey. Beekeeping is regarded as an acceptable way of making individuals earn a decent living and it is endorsed by most governments. The prices of honey usually vary a lot. Honey also relies on the forces of demand and supply. Big honey suppliers either gain or endure aftermaths of a shortage or a flood on the other side of the world.

8. Nectar dearth

A nectar dearth means scarcity and shortage of flowers that produce nectars. This typically occurs in winter. A new beekeeper can find it difficult to define and manage a nectar dearth (particularly the ones that occur during summer). Drought, low rainfall, and excess heat cause the Nectar death that happens in the summer. The things that occur during a nectar dearth apart from the scarcity in flowers that produce nectar, is that a powerful colony might try to steal nectar from the nectar store of a weaker colony. A colony can be cut off from its food supply, there comes a war between the bees which gives predators like hornets the opportunity to attack and destroy the colony.

Another effect is the transfer of parasites from a vulnerable colony to a stronger one. This is one of the causes of a strong colony collapsing in a few weeks and then the beekeeper is left wondering what transpired. Once you a nectar dearth is detected, the following measures can be taken to protect the bees:

i. **Feed syrup to the bees:**

Do not put a feeder at the entrance of the hive. This to avoid luring other colonies to the hive. Make use of an internal feeder to store the food inside the beehive. Avoid essential oils or other products designed particularly for nectar deaths when feeding them. They will attract bees even far away. Place the nectar inside the hive and the bees will find the food.

ii. **Limit entrance to the colony:**

Cover upper openings. This is the first thing to do to protect the bees, whether they are going to be fed or not.

iii. Remove general feeders or wet frames close to the apiary.

This will avoid the stronger colonies attacking the weaker colonies.

Challenges become easier to tackle once research, learning, and experience sets in. One reason why beekeeping is an incredible hobby is that it is diverse in practice.

CHAPTER 3

HISTORY OF BEEKEEPING

For centuries, honey and fruits were mankind's only known sweets, therefore, bees and honey were predominant in most ancient societies. The Christian bible is full of references to these bees and jars of honey. Bee wax was used in art and weatherproof cloth, metal proof, and used in making writing tablets. At first, people simply hunted bees in hollow trees or caves and destroy their nests to gain access to the honey and bees' wax, but by 2,400 BC, ancient Egyptians had learned to keep bees in clays and pots and did not have to kill their colonies at harvest time.

Ancient Greeks and Romans kept bees in their own ways, even Spain had commercial apiaries. Then in the dark ages, there were little advancements in beekeeping. However, in monasteries, the only oasis of literacy at that time kept bees which were then used to produce bee wax and bee candle wax which was utilized in preserving ancient Greek and Roman texts.

During the middle ages, beginning from around 1,500 years, beekeepers started cutting trees containing bee nests and keeping the log section as hives, it was around this time that the well-known straw scarp first appeared.

When Europeans discovered America, it was recorded that the discovery of honey bees followed shortly thereafter. The actual date and location of the introduction can't be ascertained of when and how bees were introduced into North America, but by the 1640s they were well established along the eastern coast.

Many of the most profound discoveries in beekeeping were made in the 19th century. In the early part of that century, there were many experimentations to invent the perfect hive which resulted in some outlandish designs. But then the American Lorenzo Luane Langstroth observed that bees and nature maintained a space of one-quarter inch to three-eighth of an inch around their combs. Within this space, the bees will not build comb, but instead will leave it open to allow movement in the hive. By using this principle of bee space, Langstroth set up the first hive using moveable and interchangeable combs.

This breakthrough helped in no small way to the rapid growth and standardization of beekeeping in the US. Langstroth's invention was quickly followed by Wax Foundation for building standard-sized combs, a basic honey extractor, and a smoker to calm the bees. After over 100 years, these same technologies with only small changes are the industry's basic standard today, which is a testament to the endearing genius of their inventors.

EVOLUTION OF BEES & BEES KEEPING

Over 50 million years ago, bees split off from the wasp sub-order and switched from animal to plant protein. Bees and flowers coevolved since flowering plants needed mobile pollinators to procreate and the bees needed the pollen.

The connection between plants and bees can be described as part of the fundamental origin of bees and human relationships as seen in the four early ages of man and bee relationship.

The first of these early ages of man and bee relationship was the Medieval Bee-hunting Age. This is an era predominantly characterized by honey hunting by man as honey was seen as a major sweet source in the absence of or inadequacy of berries and as expected the bees were protective of their honey which was their food collected and produced over time.

Eventually, the beekeepers discovered that smoke was a vital tool in the honey collection from bees because the smoke helps in weakening or calming the bees, giving honey collectors or beekeepers easy access to the hive for honey collection.

About 4000-5,000 years back, the Egyptians were on record to be the first to make hives for bee production which were made from pottery materials. In the designed hive, the bees produced their young in one end of the designed hive, while they produce honey at the other end of the hive. Over time, the Egyptians were able to develop an industry where they would position the hives in areas where the bees can access enough nectar along the Nile River for production all year round. This instance is one of such that can be described as an evolutionary beekeeping phase in human history. Progressively, in the Northern part of Europe, it was recorded that people began a tradition of collecting swarms of bees and also started using logs bee breeding.

Since the bees were owned independently, the early people established ways of identifying and marking their bee swarms irrespective of the location the swarms were located, especially during the harvest periods. According to Prof. John Free, beekeeping in early central Europe got a big boost from the spread of Christianity because of the churches' need for candles, every rabbi and monastery had its own apiary and many of the persons who worked on rented church land also kept bees to be able to pay back part of their yearly rent in wax. Similarly, human hive building in Northern Europe followed the usual progression in the form of an evolutionary pattern of suspended logs, trees, and then they began to make Skeps which over time have been portrayed among the classiest inventions in beekeeping. This skep is a hat material made from straws designed or built in the form of an inverted bowl. These inverted woven straw baskets in the form of a bowl became widespread that it continued today to be part of the symbol of beekeeping.

The baskets were easily made and transportable. They could also be extended to accommodate the increase in the production of the honey flow, but they were not immune to the weather and gradually they evolved protective niches in stone walls called Peebles which can still be seen today in parts of countries like France, Switzerland, and Italy. By the early 17th century, a Spaniard by the name Louis Mendes and an English man by the name Charles Buttler concluded that the head of the beehive is a female and not male, which counters Shakespeare's popular assertion that the head of a beehive was a King bee as at then. Subsequently, between the 16th and 19th century, gifted amateurs struggled to get more control over the bees and figured out a way to collect the honey without killing the bees because that had been the traditional method of honey extraction from bees at the end of the season.

Even for Charles Darwin, the nature of the bees posed an intellectual dilemma as he formulated his concept of evolution, which partly focused on how infertile workers successfully reproduce and flourish. Eventually, Darwin was able to realize and conclude that natural selection may be applied to the family as well as to the individual and may thus gain the desired end. Charles Darwin brought up the idea that the hive could be considered as a super-organism with the queen at the top with about three to four hundred drones, and about fifty to sixty thousand workers in it.

Due to their observed nature, the drones are examples of what is biologically referred to as haplodiploidy which means that they have no father but have a grandfather. Honey bees were recorded to have first been introduced to Northern America, which was first put into imperfect hives. Over time, the main challenge for beekeepers became how to extract honey from beehives without killing the bees. This led to several attempts by many people to create a perfect beehive that will solve this problem.

Eventually, a congregational minister in Philadelphia by the name Lorenzo Langstroth developed an idea where he thought of constructing a wooden frame that would mimic the activities in the hive and make divisions between the combs and so that during honey extraction the frames can be easily pulled out from the hive, shake the bees off, remove the honey and put the frame back inside the hive making the bees unharmed during honey extractions.

This idea has been the foundation in which successful beekeeping has been built on. Subsequently, a German fabricated the matrix used for producing the wax through an extruder that mimicked the six-sided bee cells in which the wax can be forced into the extruder and gotten into sheets. In the 1870s, there was a Czech who invented an extractor that looks like the washing machine in which the frames can be put into and spin out the wax and honey, then it goes through the separator, and then the honey is extracted and bottled. This circulated worldwide gradually and boosted the development of the beekeeping, especially as a business. Similarly, an American from New-York by the name Moses Quinby developed or invented the Smoker which in function or by design is to calm bees, especially during honey extraction processes.

The idea behind the creation and use of smokers is a result of previous knowledge about bee mode of interaction which is primarily through smell as such using smokes to communicate makes the bees perceive the extractor as less of a threat. As time passed, there was more interest, especially by beekeepers to improve the genetic stock of keeping bees as there was a higher preference for a particular bee species called the German black bee.

In the 13th century, sugar was fifty times the price of honey, but today, honey is eight times the price of sugar.

In the late eighteenth century, two Germans recognized that bees as very important pollinators. This verdict was also established by Darwin that bees were a very vital part of plant procreation and overall productivity. Such discoveries, as well as the planting of single varieties of crops, have led to a commensurate increase in the pollination for business in the US, especially after World War Two.

For example, in California, about eighty percent of the world's almonds are produced and that's about nine-hundred thousand acres of landmass and each of the over nine-hundred thousand acres need about two hives of bees to be pollinated.

In effect, this translates into about two-thirds to three-quarters of all the bees in the US have to go to California in January to pollinate the almonds. This by chance has led to a rise of another sector in the beekeeping business which is commercial pollination of crops for farmers.

For instance, in the US, it is computed that the annual value of honey is about four-hundred million dollars, while the annual estimated prospects of pollination in the same United States are about thirty billion dollars which are about almost sixty-times the value of the honey produced by bees.

DISAPPEARING BEES

In 2006, a beekeeper in Florida lost all of his hives which caused a great mystery as to what led to the cause. The mystery led to what was described as CCD (Colony Collapse Disorder) which several theories surfaced in a bid to solve the mystery.

One such theory was that the occurrence was as a result of the introduction of new classes of pesticides in crop production practices, while another school of thought attributed it to perhaps attack by parasitic mites. Another group opined the cause to be climate change, especially due to the observation that most of the bees often left the hives and there won't be any dead bee seen around the hive.

Similarly, another theory was that the rapid development of using cell phones and through increased electromagnetic wave activities have been disrupting the navigational system of the bees which affected their ability to find forage and also route back to their respective hives.

No statement seems to depict the frustration of the disappearing act as that made by a honey bee researcher at the University of Colorado named Breed. In his statement, he said, "The bees happen to be fine in the fall, then by mid-spring they're just gone". Breed has studied and worked with bees for 35 years. He has regularly requested some new bee colonies every spring season.

But since CCD started having an impact on his bees, he has had to request more and more colonies each year. He never encountered a colony of bees just fade before 2005. Recently, it appears to occur most of the time. And by the time his colony collapse, the surrounding beekeepers' colonies also collapse as well.

The situation is now so bizarre that the Northern Colorado Association of Beekeepers now has to truck in hundreds of packages of bees each spring to replace those that have vanished.

The precise reason that's causing CCD remains a mystery. Among the initial suspects: parasites that penetrate the hives, especially the bloodsucking Varroa (Vuh ROW uh) mite.

Subsequently, a few scientists got data that related the cause to particular pesticides. Other biologists have related the situation to illnesses and infections, in which some are caused by viruses. Scientists now presume the parasites, pesticides, and infections combine to provide a threefold effect. The pesticides may initially make the bees weak. That puts the bees in a position where the bees become too weak to withstand and fight infections and pests that ordinarily would not have killed them.

Breed also asserts that the earth's change in climate makes things even worse. A climatic change can give rise to droughts or generate flooding that affects the availability of flowers on which bees rely on. This renders bees to be more susceptible than ever. Worker bees do perform duties in the hive: Nurse bees, manage, and care larvae. Forager bees collect and stack food.

A small number of guard bees safeguard the entrance of the hive from honey thieves. And some bees inspect the hive, searching for sick and dying bees. These "undertaker" bees carry the dead bees and their carcasses outside the hive. If the insects were just becoming ill, beekeepers should get their evidence near the hive.

Another reason for the fall of so many colonies is that the bees are getting lost. Christopher Connolly, a neuroscientist in Scotland who observes bees' brains speculates they may be forgetting their way home. Connolly is more curious about how pesticides affect bee brains. Honeybees can meet pesticides in several areas. People treat hives with pesticides to kill Varroa mites. Planters and gardeners treat the plants and flowers that bees feed on with chemicals to eliminate insects and other pests. Even the sugary corn syrup most beekeepers give their bees during winter can include little doses of the chemicals that planters had put to growing corn. Conolly says, most of the time, bees contact merely slight portions of these chemicals.

Typically, these contacts would be too insignificant to kill them. However, even slight doses will move round a bee's body. Approximately one-third will get to its brain.

And that may be sufficient enough to disturb the bee.

Infections, pesticides, and parasites aren't the only threat that bees face. Honeybees face another threat. Professionals from the University of Southampton, England, found out that air pollution from cars and trucks is capable of suppressing or eliminating the scent that bees trail to get food. Foraging honeybees find most flowers by fragrance.

Honeybees use the entire blend of fragrances to locate the kind of flower it prefers. When some parts of the chemicals are no longer there, bees, no longer perceive the remaining scent. Because of this, the scent that bees had been trailing to get food disappears. Pollution from automobiles can partly reduce a flower's fragrance. When bees can't locate the flower's scent, they most likely miss the food, and this can cause hunger in the colony.

EFFECT OF DISAPPEARING BEES

Bees top the list of essential species. Honey bees are generating about $30 billion a year in crops. Disappearing honeybees signify a planet without honey. They are important pollinators that perform a vital function in producing various kinds of foods including fruits. And this is because honeybees pollinate flowers and crops, thereby fertilizing the plants. Many plants will not yield fruits without pollination, also crops are used to feed livestock. This indicates that a planet where bees don't exist could strive to maintain the entire human race of 7 billion.

Fewer bees could consequently mean limited kinds of foods. All the plants that bees usually pollinate will not be fertilized, we will lose the livestock that eats those plants. Pollination is so essential to the extent that several farmers rent bees from commercial hives.

In agricultural regions, disappearing honeybee colonies may present a serious challenge to crop fertilization and the supply of food. However, another research at Rutgers University, New Brinswick named Rachael Winfree proposes that disappearing honeybees might not pose a serious threat to all farmers equally. According to her, in her region, farmland is usually in places where there are wild pollinators. Plants that are fertilized by a various combination of pollinators yield more fruit than those pollinated by a few species. The wild bees are particularly very important. They are native bees that can't be monitored by beekeepers.

Several wild bees can pollinate flowers that honeybees can't pollinate. For example, a bumblebee does a better job of pollinating tomatoes than honeybees. Furthermore, bees are not the only pollinators, moths, bats, and critters help in transporting pollen.

RECOMMENDATIONS FOR DISAPPEARING BEES

While experts investigate and research for pesticides that are safer for bees, the general population can support bees by planting native flowers and leaving uncultivated areas in our gardens. Native bees usually nest in such places.

This will help to make sure more bees will be available for the next season. All the researchers advise limiting or avoid using pesticides around our homes. The best way they can do this is to employ integrated pest management which is more helpful and favorable for the environment. Pesticides won't go away completely. They ensure that pests won't destroy the crops on which people depend for food.

CHAPTER 4

PROCESS OF BEEKEEPING

Setting up a beehive

In setting up a beehive the first challenge is determining where to place the hive. All the important equipment, including parts of the hive, the smoker, and the hive tool, can be purchased online from an online shop. It's better, to begin with, new equipment, to avoid any unknown issue.

Stage 1: Place the Bees in Brood Box

To makc room for the bees, remove some frames from the brood box. It's essential to spray the bees with sugar water to ease and make them ready to stay in their new hive. With a few shakes of the brood box, most of the bees will find their way into the hive.

Stage 2: Replace the Frames

After placing the bees in the brood box, begin to put the frames back into the box slowly to avoid injuring any of the bees. Put the last of the frames into the box.

Stage 3: Place the Queen

Displace a plug in one end of the queen's cage and replace it with a bit of marshmallow, make sure that the worker bees feed on the treat.

Exposing the bees to the queen's pheromones will make the bees recognize her. The cage is attached between two frames at the center of the wooden box.

Stage 4: Feed the Bees

The inner cover should be placed on top of the brood box. It's important to feed the bees with a 2:1 sugar-water solution while the house is being set up. Minute holes on the lid of the jar give access to the bees gets the liquid. Proceed to feed them with the sugar-water solution until they start relying on the area's spring nectar flow instead.

Stage 5: Finish Assembly

The feeder is housed by the second box. Once the roof of the hive is put in place, allow the bees to stay on their own for about three to five days. After the 3-5 days come back to ensure that the queen has been released.

DETERMINANTS OF A HIVES LOCATIONS

The following factors should be considered when planning for a location a place for your beehive.

Availability of nectar and pollen: Honeybees can travel up to 3 miles or more while foraging for food, but they will opt to have it accessible without having to travel far to get it, at least within 300-500 yards of the hive. Locate your hive where forage will be available for them throughout the season.

Bees need easy access to water: Bees like every other insects and animal need water to live. They drink water, they also use water to liquidity crystallized honey, and to produce beebread which they use in feeding their larvae. Create an artificial bird bath close to the hives if no natural source of water is available.

Exposure to sunlight: Hives should face south with a reasonable dose of southern exposure and also, a biased shade, or dotted sunlight can be good for the hive especially during the summer peak.

Protection from wind: Set up the hives against small trees, or set it at the perimeter of a forest, place the hives along with a shack, cabin, or other outbuildings so that colonies will be protected from strong persisting winds. This is particularly necessary for people living in regions where winter can send cold and sharp winds to hives.

Keep the hives dry: Bees are vulnerable and sensitive to fungal diseases that are prominent in wet places. So, select a dry location for the hives and make sure it has a good drainage system in case of extended rainy periods. Also try leaning the hives forward a little bit so that the moisture that accumulates inside the hives flows out of the hive, instead of dripping down on the bees.

Protect colonies from harmful pesticides: Insecticides, herbicides, and fungicides influence the health of honeybees in one way or another. Site your hive in a location where there no threats of chemicals to ensure good health for the bees.

The proximity of human activities: Site your beehive away from commercial places and places where humans perform activities. Do not site the hive in places that are near to schools, markets, hospitals, playgrounds, highways, etc. because bees can attack and sting humans.

In summary, determining the location for beehives is very necessary for successful beekeeping. Bad siting of a beehive can cause decreased honey production and an increased cost of production. Also, not siting it properly can cause conflicts with humans because of the threat from bees. Therefore, it is important to determine the factors that will enhance the health and activities of bees for increased honey production. A properly sited beehive is long-lasting and beneficial over long periods.

BREEDING BEES

Bees like every other creature possess both good and bad traits which can be passed from one lineage to another lineage. It is typical of agriculturists to select the best traits in farm animals and insects. Inbreeding better bees, female (queen), and male (drones) bees are required. The Queen from a strong colony is ideal to mate with the desired drone. The gene of the drones can't be entirely controlled. The best way to influence the gene is to saturate the area with healthy drones from colonies with preferable qualities.

Regardless of how you want to raise queens, be sure to give your queen-rearing system opportunities. Limit the use of chemical treatments and ensure that bees have lots of pollen and honey. While selecting traits, one thing to note is that some traits are more hereditable than others. Inbreeding, most of the preferable and suitable traits to look for in the case of honey bees include:

Disease resistance: Bee breeders are improving in breeding bees that can resist and withstand diseases even more. This can be achieved by selecting from strong colonies that need fewer treatments.

Hardiness: Winter hardiness is particularly crucial to beekeepers in environments that have extended, and frigid winters. A winter with a deep freeze that lasts for 10-12 weeks isn't friendly and can affect bees' survival. Breed from healthy and strong colonies that can withstand a long cold spell must be healthy and strong. These strong colonies produce enough honey to last them during winter. And they reduce rearing brood in the fall and begin during spring to increase their numbers so they can benefit from the spring nectar flow. A strong, productive, and healthy colony can withstand a northern winter, and these are good and preferable traits.

Gentleness: Gentleness is an essential trait that bees need to possess because no beekeeper will want to get stung. It is very beneficial as well. Gentleness in a colony can be tested by actively waving a wand with a black leather patch at the edge over a hive. This will panic the bees, and they may go to sting the leather patch. In about 2 minutes or less, count the stingers attached to the leather patch. The colonies that strung lesser than the others are the gentlest.

Productivity: The production of honey is more dependent on environmental factors like weather, rainfall, etc. Genetics does not affect honey production, but for a colony that produces more honey than the other, the queen of that colony can be assessed for breeding.

Baiting and colonization

Many beekeepers worldwide rely on natural swarming to fill their hives. Swift colonization of hives requires a lot of beehives in the area. Bees have to locate the beekeepers' planned site and then to choose that it is the best spot in the area for them to use as their home. Hive colonization is relatively easy as a result because of the ecological nature of the environment. Whenever natural resources are disturbed or destroyed, the wild colonies are destroyed and this affects the colonization of beehives and also, the production of crops and biodiversity in that area. Setting and baiting beehives to lure colonizing swarms will differ and be determined by the environment. However, there will be specific standards that will be beneficial to every beekeeper who intends to develop bee colonies. In the first illustration, regardless of if it is a natural nesting site, or, beehives that are to be colonized, if they have formerly been colonized by bees then it won't be as desirable as a hive that is fresh and new. This is because bees being able to perceive the previous odors of bees that resided there before.

The fairly fresh parts of a dead bee colony and the honeycomb that was used for raising the generation are also incredibly desirable and attractive. Nevertheless, this may be harmful to the bees as it can be infested with the disease. Also, they are shortly engulfed by wax moth cocoons which makes it unattractive and unable to use for an extended period of time. Bees are particularly excited by beeswax so lots of beeswaxes should be utilized in baiting the hives.

A new starter piece of beeswax on the top-bar of a portable comb hive can attract a swarm. Some specific kinds of substances are more desirable to bees than others. It has been discovered that traditional hives are rapidly colonized than top-bar or frame hives. Plastic beehives and other man-made materials are usually unattractive while some kinds of wood can possess a strong odor that is likely to be repugnant to bees. Scorched wood, where hives where blazed to eliminate infection and pests, typically appear to have more interest, maybe because of the minerals accessible to scouting bees. A few indigenous plants can be used as attractants, especially the ones that have a lemon fragrance e.g. lemongrass. Most people have tried palm wine, banana skins, and cassava flour among the other possible items that may have varying levels of success in attracting them, but it will lure ants except the hive is properly arranged. Indigenous knowledge is one of the biggest assets to a new beekeeper because it is usually the local beekeepers that have the most appropriate reasonable knowledge to share.

The size of the cavity, swarm catcher, or hive also determines how attractive it is. The size varies with the bees' size. Smaller honey bee species like Apis cerana or African Apis mellifera are attracted to cavities or hives that are smaller in size. Bees have been discovered to have choices about the exposure of the opening to the sun and whether the hive is located in a shady position. Temperate bees will ignore a shady place while tropical bees would want a sunny place. A practical way of swarm catching is to utilize a distinct swarm catcher box positioned along a known route for swarming or migrating bees. These paths are best recognized by observing it or by conversations with local beekeepers. Once the bees have been colonized the swarm catchers can be taken to the primary beehive. Just the combs should be transferred if a portable comb or frame hive is used while the swarm catcher can be used to accumulate another swarm again.

DISEASES AND PESTS OF BEES

Maintaining and making beehives active and strong is a vital aspect of modern beekeeping. Modern beekeeping has challenges and requires a great deal of learning. Some degree of occasional losses should be anticipated. Beekeepers should always be observant and watchful about the situation and condition of their colonies.

Varroa Mites: Varroa Mites are the major enemies of honey bees and beekeepers worldwide. These parasites are external parasites and they reproduce on the pupae of honey bees and extract blood from the bees. They can greatly weaken individual bees. Mites circulate between the bee colonies through robbing. They have a high capacity to reproduce and this makes these mites difficult to manage and control by beekeepers. Most of the various treatments for varroa mites are entirely effective and numerous.

Tracheal Mites (Acarapis woodii): These parasites inhabit and grow within the tracheal tubes which are used by the insect for breathing. Destructive infestations can wreck the health of the colony negatively, but as a consequence of their microscopic stature, tracheal mites are usually disregarded by many beekeepers. Heightened distress in selection has enhanced the honey bees' biological conflict with this pest. Furthermore, the majority of the recent fumigants for the beehive that are used to fight varroa mites also regulate tracheal mites.

Aethina tumida (SHB): This tiny hive beetle is an intrusive pest of beehives. It was initially discovered in sub-Saharan Africa. The beetles reside in almost every honey bee colony in their local region, but they do minor havoc there and are hardly regarded as a terrible pest of the hive. It is unknown how this pest located the U.S but it was initially detected to be wrecking the colonies of honey bees in Florida in the year 1998. Since then it has spread to over 30 states, prevailing especially in the Southeast. The beetles have reasonably been transferred by bees packaged by migratory beekeepers. The adult beetles are powerful fliers and can travel several miles on their own.

In Arkansas the beetles are normally regarded as a minor or opportunistic pest, merely inflicting outrageous destruction after bee colonies have already become overwhelmed or weakened by other conditions. Beetles Infestations is capable put notable anxiety on bee colonies, combined with the stress of varroa mites and other diseases. If wide populations of beetles accumulate, even strong and healthy colonies can be overpowered within a short duration.

Honey bee colonies seem to be able to compete with relatively wide populations of adult beetles with minor impact. Nevertheless, large beetle populations possess the ability to lay numerous eggs. These eggs develop rapidly, which causes speedy wreckage of vulnerable combs in a short period of time. There is no specified limit for small hive beetles, because of their capacity to destroy a bee colony which is associated with the vitality, stamina, and the entire health of a colony. By keeping healthy bee colonies and maintaining a low adult beetle population, beekeepers can limit the potential of the bees to reproduce.

Wax Moths: The great Wax Moth (Galleria mellonella) is another pest that exists in honey bee hives, and inflict critical damage to honeycombs. The best way to protect bees from wax moths is to make sure that the bees are active, strong, and healthy. Once the excess combs are taken away from a hive, they should be safeguarded from wax moths until the initial hard freeze of the fall. Combs can be maintained and defended by fumigating them or keeping them in a healthy environment.

American Foulbrood (AFB): This disease is a highly deadly and infectious disease of honey bees, which is inflicted by the spore-forming bacteria Bacillus larvae. The disease makes the larvae to die after cells are capped. Worker bees find it difficult to take out the already dead larvae, moreover, they continuously infect the hive with additional spores. As the colony becomes suppressed and starts dying, bees from both close and far colonies will likely steal the honey that's left. As they move around through the hive, they become infected as well and then introduce the bacterial spores to their colony. Antibiotics do not destroy or prevent these bacteria completely, it just simply suppresses it temporarily. Colonies that have been discovered to be contaminated with the American Foulbrood disease must be eliminated by burning to avoid the disease spreading to other hives and close apiaries. Beekeepers who are skeptical of their hive being infected with AFB should reach the apiary inspectors in their state immediately. Negligence can put their hives and others around the area at risk. AFB is not fatal to humans. It is dangerous to bees only.

European Foulbrood: This is another bacterial disease that is slightly less infectious than AFB disease. A colony can recover from

EFB if it is detected at an early phase. Antibiotics can be used to treat European foulbrood disease. Modern modifications in federal law stipulate that animal antibiotics can exclusively be procured with a valid veterinary feed directive just like a prescription.

Nosema: Nosema is a disease caused by the microsporidia Nosema apis or Nosema cerana. This microorganism damages the cells in the wall of a honey bee's stomach. It reproduces and damages the cell wall continuously, finally damaging the lining of the stomach. The progression of this disease takes some time to pile up, during this time, bee finds it difficult to digest food progressively. Therefore, the bees become vulnerable and their hind-guts occupied with fecal material. Nosema disease has previously been associated with the long-lived overwintering bees, constrained in the hive for a prolonged period. Intense dysentery symptoms may become obvious in the beehive and around the entrance especially if you are unable to clean flights periodically (due to cold weather). Housecleaning practice of healthy bees usually makes them take in spores, which causes their infection. Generally, the disease fades once spring weather permits for regular cleansing flights, and spring pollen plants cause an increase in brood rearing. Nevertheless, new strains seem to be more contagious and may wreck a colony any time of the year, particularly if the colony's health has been jeopardized by exposure to pesticides.

Chalkbrood: This a brood disease that is caused by the fungus Ascophaera apis. Beekeepers commonly discover the disease in early spring when workers take out infected larvae close to the entrance of the hive. There is no medical treatment for chalkbrood disease, and it is rarely severe to the colony. As spring brood rearing improves, a colony naturally outgrows the condition If it continues year after year in certain colonies, beekeepers should remove the combs and disinfect woodenware before establishing a new foundation.

Sacbrood Virus: This virus has impacts on only the honey bee larvae, and is slightly infectious within the hive. Generally, the disease can be resisted by getting a new queen in a colony. The break in the brood cycle permits

121

worker bees to take out all infected larvae within a short time when no more larvae of a vulnerable age exist. There is no medical cure for sacbrood.

Several viruses negatively affect honey bees. A few, such as Deformed Wing Virus generate noticeable symptoms, but most do not. Presently, there is no medical cure for bee viruses. But managing the population can greatly reduce the impact of bee viruses.

Chapter 5

PROCESS OF HONEY PRODUCTION

Honey is a syrupy sweet substance generated from the nectar of flowers by honeybees. It is used as a sweetener and spread. Honey is comprised of 17-20% water, 76-80% glucose, and fructose, pollen, wax, and mineral salts. Its texture and color depend on the type of flower the bees get the nectar from. For instance, alfalfa and clover generate white honey, heather generates a reddish-brown, lavender generates an amber hue color, and acacia generates sainfoin, a straw color

Raw Materials

A typical bee colony generates 60-100 lb. (27.2-45.4 kg) of honey each year. Colonies are split by a three-tier organization of labor: 50,000-

70,000 workers, one queen, and 2,000 drones. Worker bees merely live for 3-6 weeks, each of them gathering about one teaspoon of nectar. A pound of pure honey expects 4 lbs. of nectar, which requires two million flowers to collect.

When the worker bees are up to 20 days old, they fly away from the hive to gather nectar (the sweet substance secreted by flower glands). The bee perforates the flower's petals and extract the nectar out with its tongue and keeps the nectar into its honey sac or abdomen. As the nectar moves round the bee's body, water is extracted and into the bee's intestines. The bee's glandular system secretes enzymes that make the nectar better.

Pollen fastens to the bee's legs and hairs during pollination. Some of it drops off into flowers and some blends with the nectar. When the worker bee cannot gather more nectar, she retires to the beehive. The nectar is kept in an empty honeycomb cell. Some worker bees ingest the honey, enhancing it with more enzymes which further ripens the honey. When the honey is fully ripe, it is placed into a honeycomb cell and topped with a delicate layer of beeswax.

THE MANUFACTURING PROCESS

Harvesting surplus honey is an indication that the year was a good year with adequate rainfall, which kept the flowers blooming and allowed the bees to fly.

You've fostered and pampered your honeybees till they mature. Now that the hive is busy, you can use these steps to harvest your honey.

Body Amor: Sheathe your body with bee-fortified armor for safety, especially if you're harvesting for the first time. Wear gloves that have an elbow-length and wear a veiled hat constructed for apiculture. Also, wear a bee-proof overall coat. This will protect your body and the bees from a tragic rivalry.

To take out the honeycombs, the beekeeper should wear a veiled helmet and protective gloves. There are different processes for removing the combs. The beekeeper may just brush the bees off the combs and lead them back into the hive.

Another way is that the beekeeper inserts a gust of smoke into the hive. The bees, realizing the presence of fire, force themselves on honey to take as much as they can with them before fleeing. In this case, the bees have less potential to sting when the hive is opened.

A third process requires a separator board to separate the honey section away from the brood section. When the bees in the honey section realize that they have already been detached from their colony queen, they go through another path that permits them to go into the chamber for broods, but not go into the chamber of honey again.

The separating board is deposited nearly two to three hours before the honeycomb is to be taken out. Most of the cells in the comb should be capped. The beekeeper assesses the comb by shaking it. If the honey streams out, the comb is inserted again into the honey chamber for some more days. Almost one-third of the honey is abandoned in the hive to nurture the colony.

Uncapping the honeycombs: Uncapping involves taking off the thin beeswax that is coating the honey frames to allow the honey to be exposed. When uncapping you wouldn't want to do any damage to the frames, because the drawn comb can be used again to enable you to refill the box. Honeycombs that are at least two-thirds capped are deposited in a transport box and carried to a room that is totally free of bees. Making use of a long-handled uncapping fork, the beekeeper shaves the caps from both sides of the honeycomb into a capping tray. The coating of wax that you grate or remove your honey frames is called cappings. Make sure you drain the honey away from the cappings and include it in your honey harvest. The beeswax you drain out can be cleaned with water and stored in a refrigerator to later thaw into beeswax cakes.

Extracting the honey: The honeycombs are injected into an extractor, a big drum that uses centrifugal force to bring out the honey. Because the entire combs can weigh as much as 5 lb. (2.27 kg), the extractor is turned on at a slow speed to avoid the combs from cracking. As the extractor spins, the honey is drawn-out and up against the walls. It falls slowly to the cone-shaped ground and out of the extractor through a spigot. Placed under the spigot is a honey bucket that is capped by two sieves, one coarse and one fine, to hold up wax particles and other residues. The honey is then dropped into drums and then it is carried to the commercial distributor.

Processing and bottling: When it is with the commercial distributor, the honey is put into some tanks and heated to 120°F (48.9°C) to melt away the crystals. Furthermore, it is kept at that temperature for a whole day. Any non-essential bee parts or pollen rise to the top and are removed. Most of the honey will be flash heated to 165°F (73.8°C) and filtered through a paper, then flash chilled back down to 120°F

(48.9°C). This procedure is executed very promptly, in around seven seconds. Although the process of heating lessens some of the honey's beneficial properties, consumers generally prefer the lighter and brightly colored honey.

A small percentage, possibly 5%, is left unfiltered. The honey looks dark and cloudy, but this unprocessed honey can be marketed in some places.

The simplest method for the starter to bottle honey is to bottle it with a plastic bottle with an opening at one end. You can effortlessly fill the bottles you want to sell, store or even give out.

When the sales of your honey start thriving, contemplate getting a heated bottle and possibly, a mechanical filler. Also, use neat, disinfected bottles and containers to prevent contaminated honey products.

MARKETING HONEY

Marketing is a proactive technique of recognizing and satisfying the needs of customers or buyers in a way that benefits them. Selling is barely the fundamental transaction which is the trading of product and profiting in return. With this definition, this means that

marketing calls for extra and careful strategizing and more calculated decision making than selling.

Beekeeping provides the opportunity for even poor people to harvest commercial and retail products that they can generate income from. The popular bee products called honey can be sold in a suitable market. Beekeepers should determine the market that suits their products most. Beekeepers can only make this decision when the society understand the ready options available. Opportunities in the market differ because of the amount of honey ready to be sold and the wide opportunities convenient to the beekeeper for evaluating a certain market and this is determined by area, connections, and available resources to do marketing.

For instance, a beekeeper who has just a small quantity of honey ready just after harvesting and who is not able to move to an area where there is less honey on the market will have lesser options for the market. The chance is that the only choice will be the local market and the local price. A beekeeper who is capable of storing honey until others are done selling will have a reasonable local market with literally a higher price for the honey as it will be scarce. On a bigger scale, a beekeeper with a lot of colonies who can pay for the transport for the honey will be able to get access to more distant retail markets. Beekeepers who have only a modest amount of honey to trade, but who are willing to join up with other beekeepers in the same position - perhaps to pay for transport to new markets will have various choices again.

Generally, local markets offer a little amount of regular cash income but have a limited chance for growth of the beekeeping enterprise. This is mostly true if more beekeepers are trying to sell in the local market at the same time. Inaccessibility to distant markets and glutted markets might make the producers susceptible to middlemen giving less money than the producers had hoped for, thereby discouraging them to continue to be interested in the further production of honey.

Distant markets can assimilate larger volumes of honey so that they can produce considerable wealth for the producers. Regardless, these markets need far more volumes of honey and usually require a reliable supply throughout the year.

This continually needs co-operation between many different people to make up a supply chain. The more remote the market is, the more extended the chain of supply will be. Like every chain, this will consist of several links (producers, sellers, wholesalers, and retailers).

If any of the links in the chain break out or is omitted, then the entire chain of supply will crumble. It should be known that each link in the marketing chain in honey will want to profit from the sale of the honey which may influence both the buying and selling price. Remote markets need larger volumes, reliable time of delivery, established quality standards, and probably have some regulatory responsibility.

STORING HONEY

Honey is one of the simplest substances to store. Just store it in a tightly sealed container in a cool place away from direct sunlight. Use the initial bottle the honey came in. Any glass jar or food-safe plastic container is recommended. Do not store honey in metals so it won't oxidize.

It is not mandatory to store honey in a refrigerator. It's considerably easier to use if it's not refrigerated because the cool condition will make the honey to thicken. This makes it hard to use it at your own time and it will need to be heated to a liquid stage before it can be used.

Honey can also be frozen, though this isn't mandatory. Also, avoid heat and moisture. The most hazardous thing that can happen to honey is to open it to a hot temperature and letting moisture enter the container.

Regular room temperature is suitable. If your house usually gets hot, get a cool place in the pantry to keep your honey. Furthermore, keep it far away from sunlight, stove, or, any equipment that produces heat.

To prevent moisture from entering the honey, seal the honey container tightly and take from a container with a dry spoon. Just a little quantity of water can enable fermentation, which is how the mead is brought about. For your kitchen use, this is not ideal, and it can lower the value of your honey.

SHELF LIFE OF HONEY

Honey has an incredible extended shelf life. Honey has a high level of sugar and it's one of the most durable natural foods that exists. It can retain an almost unlimited shelf life if it's stored appropriately. Honey producers usually put 2 years on the tag. This is done for functional purposes because honey differs a lot.

Nevertheless, they do point out that honey can be durable for years and even centuries. Realistically, the shelf life of honey is determined by how it's manufactured, i.e. if it is pasteurized or raw, how it is packaged, how it is preserved, etc.

Some natural chemical alterations can happen, so it might become dark or crystallize and also lose some of its taste and scent over time, but it is unlikely to go bad.

Do not be surprised or shocked if your honey turns cloudy while it's being stored. This is called crystallization. It is not detrimental neither is it a sign of decay. Pure raw honey with an increased amount of pollen will crystallize rapidly than most honey produces commercially.

Frigid weather also causes crystals. Crystallized honey is one of the several forms deliberately produced by many beekeepers because it can be preferable at times.

If honey is in a crystallized form, it is easy to re-liquify it. Just put the jar of honey in a bowl or pot of heated water and turn it while it's heating.

Do not allow it to overheat it because excess heat can distort the taste and color when the sugars start to caramelize. Also, do no use a microwave because microwaves can get heated too fast.

If you can't use a stove, use a pot of heated water rather. Though it may take time to turn into a liquid state and you may have to change the heated water if it becomes too cool.

CONCLUSION

Bees are interesting creatures that have been with mankind over the ages. They produce one of man's most sought products, the honey through the process of their activities in hives. In ancient times, men went through a lot of risks to try to harvest these honey, often, the process of harvesting these kinds of honey resulted in the destruction of the bees and their hives which is why apiculture is very important because it allows hobbyist as well as farmers to manage their own farm.

Bees play a very important role in the sustainability of the planet, they are useful in pollinating flowers and many crops on the farm, they also produce honey as well as other byproducts in the process. But beekeeping is not for the faint-hearted, it takes quite a lot of courage, some element of risk, and a lot of knowledge. However, for those who take the plunge, it can be very rewarding, and many people have been able to make a living out of it.

Honey is a base product for many pharmaceutical products and is also very popular in the beauty and cream industry. The desire for honey will continue to increase and so will the demand which is why a book like this is necessary to point you in the right direction towards starting your beekeeping practice.

CPSIA information can be obtained
at www.ICGtesting.com
Printed in the USA
LVHW051146010723
751331LV00029B/896